T2-BSU-342

CITY MACHINES
ASPHALT PAVERS

Connor Dayton

PowerKiDS
press.

New York

Published in 2012 by The Rosen Publishing Group, Inc.
29 East 21st Street, New York, NY 10010

Copyright © 2012 by The Rosen Publishing Group, Inc.

All rights reserved. No part of this book may be reproduced in any form without permission in writing from the publisher, except by a reviewer.

First Edition

Editor: Jennifer Way
Book Design: Ashley Drago

Photo Credits: Cover, pp. 10, 14, 22, 24 (bottom) Shutterstock.com; pp. 4–5, 9, 13, 21 © www.iStockphoto.com/Mike Clarke; pp. 6–7, 24 (top left) © www.iStockphoto.com/Andre Comeau; pp. 17, 24 (top right) Win Initiative/Getty Images; p. 18 © www.iStockphoto.com/Robert Asento.

Library of Congress Cataloging-in-Publication Data

Dayton, Connor.
 Asphalt pavers / by Connor Dayton. — 1st ed.
     p. cm. — (City machines)
 Includes index.
 ISBN 978-1-4488-4962-8 (library binding) — ISBN 978-1-4488-5074-7 (pbk.) — ISBN 978-1-4488-5075-4 (6-pack)
 1. Asphalt pavers—Juvenile literature. I. Title.
 TE273.D39 2012
 625.8'5—dc22

                                    2010053096

Manufactured in the United States of America

CPSIA Compliance Information: Batch #WS11PK: For Further Information contact Rosen Publishing, New York, New York at 1-800-237-9932

CONTENTS

Roads are made of asphalt. Asphalt pavers lay out new roads.

First, a dump truck puts asphalt into the paver's **hopper**.

The paver heats the asphalt. Then the asphalt is laid on the road.

The tractor moves the paver.
It puts out the asphalt.

The screed shapes the asphalt. This makes it even.

13

Next a **roller** presses the asphalt. This makes it smooth.

Road crews use pavers.

17

The paver moves slowly.
The road crew follows
behind the paver.

The road crew checks the new road. It must be smooth.

21

Asphalt pavers build new roads every day!

WORDS TO KNOW

hopper   road crew

roller

INDEX

WEB SITES

Due to the changing nature of Internet links, PowerKids Press has developed an online list of Web sites related to the subject of this book. This site is updated regularly. Please use this link to access the list:
www.powerkidslinks.com/city/asphalt/

625.85 D
Dayton, Connor.
Asphalt pavers /

OAK FOREST
01/14

OAK